A YEAR IN PAARL

WITH A I PEROLD

A YEAR IN PAARL

WITH A I PEROLD

VINE & WINE

EXPERIMENTS

1916

SOME VITICULTURAL AND OENOLOGICAL
EXPERIMENTS CONDUCTED AT THE PAARL
VITICULTURAL EXPERIMENT STATION
DURING 1915-1916

BY

DR. A. I. PEROLD

EDITED, WITH AN INTRODUCTION, BIOGRAPHY,
EXPLANATORY NOTES, PHOTOGRAPHS,
GLOSSARY & INDEX

BY

PETER F MAY

INFORM & ENLIGHTEN LTD

This edition first published in Great Britain in 2011

by Inform & Enlighten Ltd

Introduction, notes, biography, photographs, glossary and this edition of Dr Perold's work are

© Copyright Inform & Enlighten Ltd 2011

ISBN: 978-0-9561523-1-2

**

INFORM & ENLIGHTEN LTD

47 FONTMELL CLOSE

ST ALBANS AL3 5HU

Also by Peter F May

PINOTAGE: Behind the Legends of South Africa's
Own Wine

Marilyn Merlot and the Naked Grape: Odd Wines
from Around the World

Peter F May is the publisher of

www.pinotage.org

and

www.winelabels.org

'May is an oenologist of some distinction'
– Satisfaction magazine

For Joan, Daniel, Toby and Ethel

and

To the Memory of

ABRAHAM IZAK PEROLD

20 October 1880 – 11 December 1941

Contents

Abandoned old stukvat

outside Whalehaven Winery, Hermanus

About this book

Abraham Izak Perold could be said to be the father of not only the modern South African wine industry but also those of brandy and table grapes. I became interested in A I Perold while researching my book on Pinotage. Up to then the only mentions of him that I had encountered were in relation to Pinotage, the wine grape variety that he bred. I soon came to realise what a pivotal role Dr Perold had played in South African viticulture.

Although Dr Perold wrote more than eighty pamphlets, article and books none of them are now in print, a situation I hope to rectify. This book contains the complete text of a pamphlet he wrote and which was published in 1916. It is Dr Perold's annual report on his work at the government viticultural research station at Paarl, near Cape Town, South Africa.

It should be noted that, unlike the northern hemisphere where spring, summer and autumn all occur during the same year, South

Africa's grape growing season commences with spring bud break in October and concludes with harvest in February—March the following year. So Perold's report for 1915-16 covers just one year's vintage.

The text has been reformatted to fit the page but otherwise remains as the original. Apart from the correction of obvious minor typographical errors the text is complete, unabridged and a faithful copy and thus old-fashioned conventions, including full-stops (periods) after abbreviations such as 'percent' have been reproduced.

Notes at the end of this book identify the few corrections made to the original text and the glossary explains the meanings of Dutch and Afrikaans words, obscure terms and also has information about grape varieties mentioned.

Acknowledgments

I would like to thank Pierre Loubser in Somerset West, Francois Naudé Snr of Chateau Naudé Wine Creation in Stellenbosch, Frans Smit, Cellar Master at Spier Wines, Stellenbosch and Jeanette Stals in Stellenbosch for their assistance.

My thanks also to Samantha Bennett at the SAWIS Wine Information Centre Library in Paarl and the staff of Stellenbosch University Library for making me welcome to use their research facilities.

The cover photograph shows recently harvested wine grapes ready to go into the destemming machine at Spier Winery.

All photographs were taken by the author, except for that of A I Perold which is copyright of The Pinotage Association and is used with permission.

Introduction

When Dr Perold sat down in 1916 to write an annual report to his masters in the Department of Agriculture events were happening that would profoundly affect South African wine and thus his future career.

Perold had been employed in 1907 by the Government of the Cape Colony with the mission to improve the quality of grape vine products: wine, brandy and table grapes. He had been sent to Europe to study wine and brandy making methods and he had travelled widely seeking out suitable varieties for growing in the Cape.

Grape farmers were suffering because of overproduction which followed replanting after the devastation of phylloxera and the collapse of export markets. Perold believed another problem was that inferior grape varieties were being grown for quantity rather than quality. All round improvement was the reason for his experiments in Paarl.

But farmers were taking action themselves. After several short lived attempts at forming localised farmers' co-operatives, Charles Kohler, a dentist turned gold-prospector turned politician who took up grape growing and winemaking after his doctor advised him to move to the country, called a meeting on 16 December 1916.

Kohler persuaded and cajoled farmers to form a national wine farmers' co-operative called the Co-operative Union of South Africa which soon developed into the Ko-operative Wynbouwers Vereniging van Zuid-Afrika, Beperkt (The Co-operative Wine-farmers' Association of South Africa Ltd.) better known as K.W.V.

KWV, with Kohler at its head, was to rule and regulate South Africa's wine industry for the next 74 years. A I Perold would join KWV as their Chief Wine Expert in January 1928, a position he held until his death in 1941.

Biography of A I Perold

Abraham Izak Perold was 35 when he wrote his report on his viticultural experiments in Paarl. He was born in the Cape on 20 October 1880, eldest son of Isaac Stephanus Perold and his wife Johanna Helena Brink. He was named for his grandfather Abraham Isaac, (1817-1875), who had been the first generation of the Perolds born in South Africa. Abraham Isaac's father had been brought to South Africa in 1814 as a prisoner of the Napoleonic wars, and he was the third son of Ronald Perot from Brittany, France.

Abraham Izak Perold went to school first at the *Gedenkschool der Hugenoten* (Memorial School of the Huguenots) in Wellington where he learned English and Dutch and made friends with other boys who shared his love of languages and who would later become prominent writers and champions of the Afrikaans language.

After Perold matriculated from Wellington in 1898 he continued his studies in mathematics, physics and chemistry at Victoria College in Stellenbosch where he achieved the degree BA *cum laude* Cape of Good Hope in

1901. He was awarded a bursary for overseas studies and, at the age of 21 he travelled to Halle an der Saale, Saxony-Anhalt, Germany to study at the United Frederick University. In 1904, he graduated with a D.Phil. in Chemistry for his thesis *'Über die Verbindungen der Wolle mit farblosen Aminen und Saueren'* (About the Blending of Wool with colourless Aminos and Acids).

Perold did not immediately return to the Cape. His father had asked him to learn French, the language of his great-grandfather, so Perold journeyed directly to Paris and continued his chemistry studies under Henri Moissan who two years later in 1906 would win the Nobel Prize in Chemistry for his work in isolating fluorine.

Perold returned home in 1906 and took a position as temporary professor with the South African College in Cape Town but the following year he entered the service of the government of the Cape Colony. He'd been away for four years living and studying in Germany and France and taking time to travel through Europe. He was now fluent in French and German, as well as Dutch and English and was competent in Italian, Spanish and Portuguese. He also became deeply involved in the movement to formalise and get legal recognition for Afrikaans, the everyday local language then popularly known as 'kitchen Dutch', that was an amalgam of Dutch and the languages of the indigenous San and Khoi peoples, those brought as slaves from the Malay peninsula and Indonesia, and Xhosa, Zulu and other black tribes.

Perold was sent back to Europe to study grape growing and wine making. Perold spent much time travelling, but he managed to find time in 1908 to marry Bertha Elisabeth Muller whom he'd met in Halle in Germany, and in 1909 he was travelling again looking for new grape varieties. Perold sourced and propagated more than 60 varieties new to the Cape, including wine grapes such as Grenache and Barbera, but mostly table grapes.

Perold was also writing articles about viticulture and winemaking and encouraging a more scientific approach to the subjects. He had more than eighty pamphlets, articles and books published in English and Afrikaans between 1906 and 1940.

At the end of 1912 Perold was appointed head of the Elsenburg Agricultural College and in 1917 he became the first Professor of Viniculture and Oenology at the University of Stellenbosch. The 1920's was a busy decade for Perold. He was breeding new grape varieties, one of which was Pinotage.

In 1927 Macmillan & Co in London published his masterpiece *A Treatise on Viticulture* and later that year he moved from the University to the position of KWV's Chief Wine Expert, a post he took up on 3 January 1928. KWV had been given sweeping powers in 1924 over the grape growing and wine making industry with the dual intentions of bettering the lot of farmers and improving the quality of wines and brandy to make them more exportable. Now Perold could use his knowledge and, with the authority of KWV behind him, exert real influence to advance the industry. He advised farmers on the appropriate grape varieties to plant and he was instrumental in improving the quality of KWV brandy.

Professor Perold died of a heart attack on 11 December 1941 while in KWV's employment. "The farmers had no greater friend," said his colleague Chris Theron, "and I will always remember how old seasoned farmers cried at his funeral."

There is no statue to Abraham Izak Perold and no biography apart from R U Kenney's *Abraham Izak Perold – Wegwyser van ons wingerdbou* which is a collection of reminisces from people who knew him. That book was published in Afrikaans in 1981 and is long out of print. Today A I Perold is mainly remembered in connection with the Pinotage wine grape variety that he bred in 1924-5.

One ton capacity upright open topped stukvats used for small scale fermentations at Spier Winery.

UNION OF SOUTH AFRICA
DEPARTMENT OF AGRICULTURE

Some Viticultural and Oenological Experiments conducted at the Paarl Viticultural Experiment Station during 1915-1916

By Dr. A. I. PEROLD
Government Viticulturist
for the Union of South Africa

Some Viticultural and Oenological Experiments conducted at the Paarl Viticultural Experiment Station during 1915-1916.

By Dr. A. I. PEROLD, Government Viticulturist for the Union of South Africa.

INTRODUCTORY

As an annual report has to be very brief, any details about experimental work have to be omitted, but these are of the greatest importance to viticulturists, and should, therefore, be brought to their notice. It is with this object in view that the present bulletin has been written.

The experiments are here grouped as follows : —

A. *Viticultural:*

(*a*) Pruning and Trellising.
(*b*) Sunburning of Grapes.
(*c*) Thinning of Table Grapes.
(*d*) Almeria Grapes.
(*e*) Local Sales of Table Grapes.
(*f*) Experimental Shipments of Export Grapes.

B. *Oenological* :

(*a*) Hock Type.
(*b*) Claret Type.
(*c*) Sherry Type.
(*d*) Port Type.
(*e*) Wine Brandy (Cognac Type).

A. VITICULTURAL EXPERIMENTS.

(a) Pruning and Trellising.— After trying different systems with over 100 different varieties of grapes for several years, it can now be stated that only such vigorous varieties as Molinera Gorda (or Meraviglia de Malaga and Castiza, with which it is practically identical), Black Manukka, White Crystal, and a few others, together with such varieties as need long pruning to give good crops, e.g. Sultana, Ohanez (Almeria), Black Currant (Cape), Karroo Belle, Cabernet Sauvignon, and a few others, answer well when trellised and pruned according to the Cazenave system. Here we have a permanent trunk on the bottom wire with 4-6 short and long (about 8-10 eyes) bearers to each vine, the long bearers being tied to the middle wire. Varieties bearing well with short pruning will give too heavy crops with long pruning, with the result that the grapes ripen badly and are of poor quality, whilst the vines at the same time suffer visibly. Most varieties of table grapes give the best results when only short bearers of 2-3 eyes are given about 9 in. apart on a permanent trunk resting on a strong (No. 8 or 10) wire with a second wire (say No. 12) about 12 in. above it. Quite sufficient quantity and very satisfactory quality are thus obtained.

The modification of the Cazenave system known as the "fish-spine method," where the long bearers are tied to outside wires. 15-18 in. away from the trunk and on both sides of it, alternately to the one and then to the other wire, gave better results than the Cazenave system in the case of Flame-Coloured Tokai, as sun-burning was thereby very much reduced. This "fish-spine method" also seems very useful for the Almeria grape (Ohanez) as well as for Sultana.

The overhead trellising (Pergola and the Almeria system) has thus far given good results in the case of table grapes. For the Almeria grape the overhead trellis gave twice as big a crop as the low trellis, even with long pruning. This trellising has thus far not given any special results in the case of wine grapes. The sugar content of these grapes when ripe was a little lower than in the case of vines not trellised, but the difference was not great. Sun-burning practically never occurs on an overhead trellis.

(b) Sunburning of Grapes. This is a serious matter in hot places like Paarl. Whilst it is certain that deep, cool soils with a loose soil mulch on the surface will cause much less sunburning than dry soils, it still sometimes happens that the air gets so hot (102-104 F. in the shade), that the grapes burn badly. This is usually worst between the 30th December and 4th January. Later on, as the grapes get sweeter and the acidity decreases, sunburning is less to be feared. Experiments made with hessian to provide artificial shade between 12 noon and

4 p.m., have given some useful results, but it is felt that this is not the real solution of the problem. *Trellising has done more than anything else.* The "fish-spine" method of trellising gave rise to much less sunburning in the case of Flame-Coloured Tokai, which is a very susceptible variety, than the Cazenave system. The experiment will now be extended to Gros Maroc, which is another variety extremely susceptible to sunburning. High and overhead trellising so far proved to be the most effective means of preventing sunburning. It will, therefore, pay well in the case of Hanepoot, Flame-Coloured Tokai, and Gros Maroc.

(c) Thinning of Table Grapes. As is well known, this is an essential factor in the production of the best table grapes. In order to determine approximately the percentage of berries that should be removed in case of the different varieties of grapes, four to thirteen bunches of grapes of a number of varieties were carefully thinned on the 30th November, 1st, 8th, and 9th December, and the number of berries removed, as well as those remaining after thinning, were counted, whence the percentage removed in each case was calculated. The results were as follows :

Variety.	Number of Bunches Thinned.	Percentage of Berries Removed.	Average
Laubscher's Gem	5	36-61,	49
Prune de Cazouls	13	23-57,	43
Henab Turki	7	40-46,	48
Trifere du Japon	4	41-53,	44
Gros Colman	6	28-52,	43
Bailey	4	48-54,	51
*Kirsten	5	64-73,	67
Barlinka	5	38-47,	42
Gros Maroc	5	40-56,	48
Bonnet de Retord	5	50-58,	53
Tribodo Nero	5	39-50,	46
Formosa	5	50-60,	53
Cinsaut	5	42-53,	48
Schiradzouli Blanc	5	37-53,	44

Subsequent results have shown that the bunches in question were properly thinned. The above table shows that in the same variety there are considerable differences between the percentages of berries to be removed from different bunches. It is, therefore, not possible to say precisely what percentage of berries should be removed in thinning each variety of grape. Still, it will be noticed that there are on the whole considerable differences between the different varieties. Thus the variety called "Kirsten," which is marked with an asterisk in the above list, needed very heavy thinning indeed as compared with the other varieties. When table grapes for export are to be produced upon a large scale, we should try to grow such varieties as do not require to have more than about 45 per cent, of their berries removed when thinning, unless they are of such great excellence as to pay well for this extra amount of work. In the above list Gros Colman, Barlinka, and Prune de Cazouls required least thinning (42-43 per cent.), and they are three excellent export varieties.

In the case of Eosaki di Smyrna and Dattier de Beyrouth, all the thinning required consisted in removing the few small berries. They, indeed, require less thinning than any other varieties known to the writer. They are excellent for export. Hanepoot requires a very variable amount of thinning. In years when the berries have set well, it will require up to 50 per cent, thinning, whereas in years when the berries have set badly, the thinning will be almost nil, and will be limited to the removal of a few small berries.

(d) Almeria Grapes. As it was felt that the Almeria grape should have a great future in South Africa, cuttings of this variety, known as Ohanez, were imported into the Cape early in 1910, through the good offices of the British

Consul in Almeria. It was in due course propagated at the Paarl Viticultural Station, where it is grown on different systems of trellising, including the Almeria overhead trellis. It was grafted on Jacquez and on Aramon, both thus far doing well. The 1915 crop, which was fairly heavy, was almost completely destroyed by the ordinary Fruit Fly.

The 1916 crop was a good one. By applying two sprays with poisoned bait against Fruit Fly on the 22nd February and 3rd March, the whole crop was saved. It would, therefore, appear that the Fruit Fly is not any serious difficulty in the production of Almeria grapes. Owing to a more favourable season, the grapes were picked on the 14th March, which was about six weeks earlier than the year before. The best results were obtained from the over-head trellis (Almeria system), where the ninety-six vines, planted 6 ft. × 6 ft., gave an average of one 10-lb. box of grapes per vine, which is very satisfactory. Half of these grapes was exported to London and fetched from 6s. to 8s. per box. The remainder was sold on the Johannesburg market as follows: —

On 20th June, 12 boxes at 5s. to 6s. per box ; on 4th July, 15 boxes at 5s. per box ; on 9th August, 9 boxes at 7s. to 8s. per box. The average price realized was 5s. 8d. per box. It must, however, be pointed out that just a little more than half of the grapes harvested for local sale could thus be sold, as there was a fair loss in keeping them so late. This would still work out at an average price of about 3s. per 10-lb.

box harvested, which is very profitable indeed. These grapes were stored in the wine cellar, some being packed in corkdust and others wrapped in paper, each bunch by itself. Neither of these methods seem to be very satisfactory. In future the Almeria grapes will be stored by packing them in single layers on fruit trays, which will be kept in a fairly cool and dry place, stacked one on top of the other. This has already been done last season by a private farmer on my advice, and was attended with very good results. I prefer this method to keeping in cold store. Future experiments will, no doubt, prove the accuracy of my contention.

Those Almeria grapes shipped to England were packed in the usual 10-lb. box (each bunch being wrapped in tissue paper by itself), and were sent over in ventilated hold, arriving in good condition. The prices realized were quite satisfactory, as was shown above. Next season some boxes will be exported with the grapes packed in corkdust, to determine which manner of packing pays best. The grapes were sold on the Covent Garden Market, London, on the 10th May. Those picked in the ampelographic collection were specially marked "A.C.," and they were on the whole riper than those picked from the overhead trellis. In his report on this consignment (40 boxes), the Trades Commissioner, Mr. Chiappini, writes as follows :

"The portion of the shipment marked 'A.C.' had a fair percentage of wasty berries. The portion which had no distinguishing mark were in quite good condition, hardly a bad berry to be found."

This simply corroborates the experience in Almeria, where the grapes are picked a bit on the green side, to make them keep longer and better. It is, therefore, advisable to pick the Almeria grape when it is just ripe, but before it is dead ripe.

(e) *Local Sales of Table Grapes.* In all 155 10-lb. boxes of a large number of different varieties of table grapes from the Paarl Experimental Station were sold on the Johannesburg market between 1st February and 25th March, 1916. The prices were uniformly satisfactory, the average price being 3s. 4d. per box. The grapes were quite ripe and of good quality, although not "extra selected." This shows that in the case of local sales it pays to put up the grapes in small parcels and to send good, ripe stuff to the markets. Growers should note this fact, and develop this line of trade, in preference to selling their whole crops of good Hanepoot and other grapes at 3s. to 4s. per basket of at least 50 lb. grapes.

(f) *Experimental Shipments of Export Grapes.* During the last export season 185 standard 10-lb. boxes of table grapes were exported from the Paarl Experimental Station to London and consigned to the Trades Commissioner, who carefully inspected each consignment, had them sold at Covent Garden, and fully reported upon the results. The following are the opening remarks in his report on these experimental shipments:

"What I consider to be the most important experiments ever made in regard to the fruit trade were those made by Dr. Perold (the Chief Viticulturist of the Government), who made several shipments including many varieties of new types of table grapes grown at the Government experimental plot at the Paarl. Great care was taken in the details of the shipments, and the results were most satisfactory. ... I personally inspected every consignment very carefully, always in company with Covent Garden dealers, and I hope the experiments will be continued next year."

These shipments comprised thirty different varieties of table grapes. On account of the small number of boxes sent of each variety (in some cases one or two only), the prices realized do not reflect the correct value of the different grapes for export purposes. The greatest value of these experimental shipments consists in the careful reports made about their travelling qualities, and the public favour that the different varieties are likely to find at Covent Garden. The following are some of the best varieties for export :

(a) Varieties already largely exported. Gros Colman, Red and White Hanepoot, Barbarossa, Hermitage, and Raisin Blanc.

(b) New Varieties, now recommended: Gros Maroc, Black Spanish, Muscat Madresfield

Court, Molinera Gorda, Olivette Barthelet, Servan Blanc, Dattier de Beyrouth, Kosaki di Smyrna, Barlinka, Prune de Cazouls, Henab Turki, Eosada, and Bonnet de Ketord.

The following list gives the prices realized by these varieties this year at Covent Garden Market. It may beforehand be pointed out that these must not be regarded as maximum prices, as they are unduly low on account of the small number of boxes, usually only two to six or even one, that could be offered for sale.

Gros Colman			15s,	average	15s.
Dattier de Beyrouth			14s.,	"	14s.
Henab Turki	10s.	to	14s.	"	12s.
Black Spanish			12s.	"	12s.
Olivette Barthelet			12s.	"	12s.
Gros Maroc	10s.	to	12s.	"	11s. 6d.
Molinera Gorda	9s.	"	13s.	"	11s. 5d.
Barbarossa	10s.	"	12s.,	"	11s. 4d.
Rosaki di Smyrna			11s.,	"	11s.
Servan Blanc	10s.	to	12s.	"	11s.
Red Hanepoot	10s.	"	12s.,	"	10s. 8d.
Muscat Madresfield	9s.	"	12s.,	"	10s. 6d.
Raison Blanc	9s.	"	12s.,	"	10s. 6d.
Barlinka	10s.	"	12s.,	"	10s. 4d.
Prune de Cazoula	10s.	"	12s.,	"	10s. 4d.
Rosada			10s.,	"	10s.
Hermitage	9s.	to	10s.,	"	9s. 3d.
Formosa	7s. 6d.	"	10s.,	"	8s. 9d.
Bonnet de Retord	8s.	"	9s.,	"	8s. 4d.

Notes on the above Varieties.

About the old standard varieties it need simply be said that Gros Colman is the best of all, and is closely followed by Red and White Hanepoot and Barbarossa. Hermitage is quite a paying variety where it is early, hardy and gives big berries. It will probably always be shipped on account of being early. Raisin Blanc, however, should steadily be replaced by Servan Blanc. Of the new varieties Dattier de Beyrouth and Rosaki di Smyrna are two large oval-berried white varieties, that carry very well and fetch very good prices. They are mid-season varieties. This year a lot of the berries of Rosaki showed a tendency to drop off when arriving on the market, on account of the long voyage and the thin stalks of this grape. They deserve to be grown to a very considerable extent.

Henab Turki is a late grape that carries very well indeed, and forms big, nearly round berries with a pitch black colour when properly ripe. It is late but bears well, and is one of the coming varieties if grown on early sites. Mr. Chiappini writes about this variety that "dealers thought very well of this variety, and along with 'Molinera Gorda' is one of the best out of the whole experiments. It should prove a very fine export grape, but further experiments should be made."

Black Spanish.— This is a variety of considerable merit. Its berries are large, black, and of fairly good flavour. It is a very good cropper and most of the bunches are fit for export. Its cultivation can safely be encouraged.

Olivette Barthelet is a very promising new white variety. It forms fairly big bunches with good-sized berries. It travels better than Raisin Blanc, and has a firm flesh, while the berries cling to the stalks well. This grape made a good impression on the Covent Garden trade. One box was kept in the show window of the Trades Commissioner for thirteen days, when the grapes were still in good condition.

Servan Blanc is a very late white grape that gives beautiful bunches with fair-sized berries, and will probably altogether take the place of Raisin Blanc, to which it is decidedly superior. The average price realized was 11s. per box, notwithstanding the fact that this variety had not been thinned out previous to shipping. It is largely grown in the south-east of France as a late-keeping white grape. Its cultivation can be strongly recommended.

Gros Maroc is an excellent large-berried black grape that will in course of time very closely come up to Gros Colman both in quality and price. Its great drawback, however, is that it burns very easily. It should, therefore, be grown on high trellises or possibly on the fish-spine trellis, or in districts where sunburning is not to be feared. It travels really well, and is a most excellent grape for export.

Molinera Gorda.— This is a red grape with round berries and large bunches; it is a vigorous grower and good cropper. It never suffers from sunburning, ripens as early as Hermitage, and will last throughout the export season. It possesses excellent keeping qualities, as is shown by the report of the Trades Commissioner in London, where he states the following:

> "It arrived in excellent condition, and apparently is a marvellous keeping grape. The berries cling on exceptionally well, and I might almost say that not more than one berry in five bunches dropped during the inspection. One box was placed in my office show window for thirteen days, after taking seven days in coming from the ship, making a total of twenty days in all. I carefully examined the grapes afterwards, and there was hardly a berry affected in the whole box."

The grapes had thus been cut from the vines about seven weeks ago. Mr. Chiappini further adds: "I think this variety will prove an excellent one for export, and dealers here are much impressed with it." As it is further a variety that will give fairly big berries with a little thinning, it could be grown on a fairly large scale, to be shipped as "selected," and will still make good prices. This season the average price was 11s. 5d. per box. It can be strongly recommended to all growers, as it is easy to please and will succeed in early as well as late districts. This grape is exported from Almeria in Spain during the four weeks preceding the exportation of the Almeria (Ohanez) grape from this district.

Muscat Madresfield Court. This is a very good cropper, suffers little from sunburning, ripens mid-season, has a nice muscat flavour (which is much liked at Covent Garden, where it is well known), and Mr. Chiappini thinks that shipments of this grape should be encouraged.

Barlinka.— This is a beautiful black grape, with strong bloom. It is at present little known, and was specially imported by myself from a small village in Algeria. Mr. Chiappini writes about this grape as follows :

> "This is an extremely nice black grape, and arrived in very good condition. The berries clung on well, whilst the flavour was quite good. This will probably prove to be a very saleable variety. It made from 10s. to 12s. per box."

Its cultivation is strongly recommended.

Prune de Cazouls is a very large-berried black Sicilian grape, which bears well and forms about the largest berries amongst the black varieties. It is very easy to thin, and is a vigorous grower. This variety will probably always command a good price, and should, therefore, be tried by growers of export grapes.

Rosada is a red variety that is exported from Almeria together with the Molinera Gorda. As the name shows, it has a rose or pink colour. The berries are very firm, and it is a peculiar, pretty grape. It travels well, and Covent Garden dealers think that it will possibly take on there when it becomes better known.

Bonnet de Retord is a peculiar striped black grape, very firm flesh and tough skin, the berries sticking very well to the pedicels. It is an excellent traveller and beautiful keeper. Where the soil is good and not too dry, the berries will reach a good size for export. The flavour is quite good. It is a deserving variety that might be tried by exporters.

B. OENOLOGICAL EXPERIMENTS.

(a) Hock Type. In these experiments two different methods were tested. First the method whereby the grapes are crushed, immediately pressed in the freshly crushed state, and the combined must is pumped into a stukvat, where it is allowed to ferment by an addition of about 1 per cent. pure yeast. The temperature during fermentation is controlled by cooling the must when necessary. As far as possible the temperature is kept below 90 F. or 32 -2 C.

The other method consists in adding about ½ lb. potassium meta-bisulphite to the must got from 1 ton of grapes by crushing and pressing immediately afterwards. The must is pumped into a cement tank, where it is left for 36 to 48 hours when the clear supernatant liquid is siphoned or pumped out, immediately pumped into a stukvat, and about 1 per cent, pure yeast is added. This second process was only tried in the case of White French grapes.

No difficulty was experienced in either case with the fermentation. Sometimes, particularly during hot weather, the must had to be cooled by pumping through a cooler. In four to six days the young wine was usually dry.

The acidity of the must was corrected by adding sufficient tartaric acid to raise the total acidity of the must to about 7 per mille. Latterly the acidity has not been raised beyond 6 per mille, as 7 per mille was found to be rather too high. The- wine was racked for the first time about eight days after pressing, then again about one month later, and again towards the end of winter, some time in August. The wines were matured in two-leaguer stukvats, which were closed by means of big perforated rubber bungs, into which fitted special glass vessels, which again were closed by a perforated cork with a bent glass tube containing a little dilute sulphuric acid to act as an airseal. This is an excellent arrangement. The cask is filled completely, until the wine nearly fills the glass vessel on top of the cask. In this way one can see, when walking through the cellar, whether the casks have been properly filled up. If an unexpected fermentation should suddenly set in, the cask will not burst, as the gas can escape through the airseal. In this way very excellent wines were made from Greengrape and White French. When 2½ years old, these wines were perfectly bright without having been either fined or filtered. They had a nice bouquet and were much appreciated by wine merchants.

The second method gave a wine much resembling the Witzenberg wine, with a distinct Moselle character about it. On the whole, both methods are equally good in normal years. Only

46

when the grapes reach the cellar in a somewhat decomposed state owing to rainy weather, the second method will be the better of the two. The great secret is to get the wines dry soon, and subsequently to fill the casks once or twice a week so as always to keep them quite full. In order to do this, pure yeast, a good cooler, and the glass vessels for keeping the vats full, are strongly recommended.

(b) Claret Type. Past experience has shown that a good, dry, red wine for table use cannot be made from Hermitage in the Paarl district. Therefore Cabernet Sauvignon (about 550) and Malbec (about 450) vines were planted in 1914. They gave their first crop during the 1916 vintage, when in their third leaf, and thus 2½ years old. The crop was 113 baskets grapes or about 2⅓ leaguers wine from the 1000 vines. This was a good yield from such young vines. The Malbec yielded about 40 per cent, more heavily than the Cabernet.

The musts had the following composition :

	Sugar in degrees Balling.	Total Acidity as Tartaric Acid.
Cabernet Sauvignon	24.0°	6.8 mille
Malbec	22.2°	6.8 mille

The grapes were crushed in a fouloir-égrappoir, which removed the stalks. The husks and the must were inoculated with pure yeast when the grapes had been crushed. The floating cake of husks was pressed under the must by means of a pole with two cross-sticks. This was done every couple of hours for about 10 minutes. After 3½ days or about 84 hours, the wine was drawn off and the husks were immediately pressed, and the press wine added to the rest. The wine was then almost dry. It was stored in a stukvat and further treated in the usual way. It soon got bright and developed a pleasant bouquet with something of a Claret character. It has a splendid dark red colour. On the 9th June, 1916, it was analysed, and gave the following results :

Alcohol.	Total Acidity (as Tartaric Acid).	Volatile Acid (as Acetic Acid).
12.40 vol.%	5.3 mille	0.52 per mille

The vines are planted 3 ft. × 8 ft., are trellised low (two wires), and pruned with long and short bearers (Guyot system), as is practised in the Medoc (Bordeaux district), where they form the basis of the Clarets. The results, both as regards quantity and quality, are thus far very encouraging. Further experiments will be continued in this direction. So much is now already certain, that these two varieties can produce quite a good, dry, red table wine in the Paarl district.

(c) Sherry Type. Experiments have in the past been made with Stein, Greengrape, and Pedro Jimenez (the false Pedro). The Sherry varieties have only come into bearing last season, so that nothing can thus far be said about them. Of the varieties first mentioned, Stein is not to be recommended for making of Sherry. Its peculiar flavour is a drawback to the matured Sherry. Greengrape and Pedro Jimenez have given good results thus far, but the Sherry made from Greengrape seems to reach a stage of maturation after about four years, beyond which it makes no marked progress, and it even seems to fall off somewhat on being further kept.

As I noticed in the ampelographic collection that the Spanish Palomino, which is the basis of Sherry in Spain, is practically identical with our White French, experiments will be made with this variety next vintage in the production of Sherry. I have recently tasted a Sherry made from White French, which was about seven years old, and had a beautiful amontillado nose and character. It is, therefore, quite likely that White French may become our main variety of grape for making a Sherry.

All my attempts to grow the flowers of wine on the young Sherries have thus far failed. I think they will succeed with White French, as it gives a wine low in both alcohol and total acid.

Meanwhile, pure cultures of *Mycoderma vini* (or Flowers of Wine) are being prepared from different young wines, that naturally tend to become good Sherries. The question as to whether plastering is necessary in the making of Sherry has not yet been decided. Experiments are still being conducted. Meanwhile it must be pointed out that about 1½ lb. plaster of paris per ton of grapes is the most that can be used, without exceeding the total sulphate limit of 2 grs. potassium sulphate per litre in the wine when ready to be sold.

My four and five years' old Sherries have developed a strong Sherry character, which is very encouraging. Most white Cape wines tend to develop into Sherries if sufficiently matured in wood, but the production of a very high-class Sherry, approximating closely to the Spanish article, will probably require a number of years and many more experiments in this direction.

(d) *Port Type.* Whereas Pontac and Muscadel in the past constituted the basis of Cape Ports, we now have over a dozen varieties of the many varieties grown in the Douro Valley in Portugal for making Port wine. One can distinguish between early and mid-season varieties. The early varieties are : Red Muscadel, Frontignac, Codega (white), Bastardo do Menudo, and Bastardo do Castello. They give very sweet must and good quality. The others come one to two weeks later, and include Tinto Cao, Mourisco de Semente, Mourisco tinto, Malvasia Rey, Malvasia preta, Grenache noir, Touriga, Tinta Francisca, and Tinta Roriz. At the

Experimental Station in Paarl it has been found necessary to press the early varieties first, and then the others. The young wines are subsequently blended. The grapes are allowed to get dead ripe before they are harvested. The early varieties gave a must with 26.5° Balling, whilst the later group showed only 22° Balling in the must.

The grapes are crushed in a fouloir-égrappoir, which crushes the grapes and removes the stalks at the same time. The husks and must are immediately inoculated with pure yeast and allowed to ferment in a cement tank. The cake of husks is pressed under repeatedly, as described under the "Claret type" above. When the Balling saccharometer shows about 8-10 degrees, the must is drawn off and the husks are pressed out. The united musts are then pumped into a stukvat containing the requisite amount of brandy, which is so calculated that there will be left about 12 in. free below the bunghole, when the necessary amount of must will have been pumped into the cask. By pumping the must on top of the brandy, the two mix well. In one to two days' time the fermentation will usually stop. After about eight days the wine is racked over into another cask, which can then be filled.

The amount of brandy required is calculated according to the following formula :

$$X = \frac{127(17 \times 17 + 10b - 10a)}{17 (s - 17) - 10b}$$

Where

X = number of gallons brandy necessary for every leaguer must.

a = number of degrees Balling of the must.

b = the percentage sugar that the finished wine should have.

s = the strength of brandy in vol. per cent, alcohol.

This formula works very well in practice, but has been deduced by myself from theoretical considerations. It is based on the assumption that the finished wine will have 17 vol. per cent, alcohol. This is sufficient to stop the fermentation, and keep the wine whilst maturing in the cellar. The alcoholic strength is usually raised 1 or 2 vol. per cent. higher in the trade. The brandy used in my experiments is made from ordinary sound wine which is distilled twice, the first and the last runnings being separated from the brandy, to be used in making the Port. The brandy is so distilled, to have a strength of about 74 vol. per cent., or about 30° O.P. The lowest strength allowed by law is 22° O.P., or 69 -6 vol. per cent. Great care should be taken in distilling, as a bad brandy will always harm the wine fortified with it. The following example will illustrate the formula given above.

The fresh must showed 25 Balling, the brandy was 74 vol. per cent., the Port should have 5 per cent, sugar when finished and have a strength of 17 vol. per cent, alcohol. Here $a = 25$, $b = 5$, $s = 74$.

$$\text{Therefore X} = \frac{127(17 \times 17 + 10 \times 5 - 10 \times 25)}{17 (74 - 17) - 10 \times 5} = 12.3$$

Thus every leaguer of must will require 12.3 gallons of the above brandy to give the wine wanted.

In 1915 about 2½ leaguers Port type wine were made at the Paarl Experimental Station, and in 1916 about 4½ leaguers of the same wine. Both these wines have a pronounced Port character and are most promising at present. From these experiments one can already now predict that we shall in future be able to produce very good wines of the Port type, which may possibly be exported with success in the near future. I am glad to say, that a number of farmers in the various wine districts have already acted upon my advice, and started planting the above Port varieties for making wine of the Port type.

(e) Wine Brandy (Cognac type). In order to make a first class brandy of this type, it is essential that we should start with a good, sound wine. In France Cognac is distilled mainly from the Folle Blanche grape, which has a very

high total acidity and fairly low percentage of sugar when ripe. The result is a light wine with a high total acidity. The wine is distilled from one to three months after the vintage, i.e. in cold weather, before it has had any chance of getting sour. No particular care is exercised in making this wine, but the greatest care is taken in distilling it and in maturing the Cognac.

I consider that the best brandy will be made from light wine, as we have thus a greater concentration of the vinous characteristics in the brandy than when distilling strong wine.

In 1914 the White French grapes at the Paarl Experimental Station were pressed when just ripe, and then showed 17.2° Balling and 4 per mille total acidity. The grapes were crushed and pressed immediately afterwards; the must was pumped into a stukvat, sufficient tartaric acid added to raise its total acidity to about 8 per mille, and the fermentation was started with pure yeast. The maximum temperature of the must during fermentation never exceeded 28° C. or 82.4° F., as it was cooled when necessary. The wine soon got dry and was racked from the first lees. During the latter half of April it was distilled according to the system of Cognac. The wine then had the following composition :

Alcohol.	Volatile Acid (as Acetic Acid).	Total Acidity (as Tartaric Acid.)
9.6 vol. % or 16.7 % Proof Spirit.	0.54 per mille.	8.47 per mille.

It was distilled in a small three halfaums still. First everything was distilled over until the alcoholometer showed 0 degrees. This constitutes the "brouillis" or crude brandy. This was then carefully redistilled. The first half gallon during the second distillation was kept separate and added to the second still. The good brandy was then collected until the strength of the brandy distilling over went just below 19° Cartier, when the remainder was treated as "naloop" and added to the second still. This "naloop" was collected until the alcoholometer showed 0° which means 10° Cartier, since pure distilled water shows 10° on the Cartier alcoholometer. In this way everything was carefully distilled, with the result that the 270 gallons wine gave 33¾ gallons good brandy of "Cognac type" with a strength of 67 vol. per cent, alcohol or 17.4° O.P. ; this means that eight leaguers of this wine would thus give one leaguer of brandy.

This brandy was put into a new quarter cask of Limousin oak, which had previously been well steamed. The brandy was very clean and matured fast. It was kept on the cellar loft under a thatched roof. Now it is a fine, soft brandy that can well be consumed, after having matured in French oak for about 2½ years. This brandy, which I can guarantee as absolutely pure and natural, now has a fine golden colour and a strong Cognac character. It very closely resembles the genuine French Cognac, and certainly approximates more closely to it than any other South African brandy that I have seen thus far.

After this experience I feel confident that we can produce a very fine wine brandy of Cognac type, if we only care to do so. For this purpose I most strongly recommend the White French grape, together with the grape grown in the Cognac district, namely Folle Blanche (best), Colombard, and Saint Emilion. This class of brandy could well be exported, and give a good profit to the growers. Cuttings of the varieties of grapes just mentioned can be obtained from the Government Viticulturist, Elsenburg, Mulders-vlei, C.P.

Experiments similar to the above are still being continued, and will be reported upon at a later stage.

Notes

The original document misses out 'is' in the first sentence of Paragraph A(*b*) and reads "*Sunburning of Grapes*. This a serious matter in hot places like Paarl."

Spelling of Experimental was corrected in paragraph B(*e*) "In 1914 the White French grapes at the Paarl Experminental Station..."

Perold's document uses 'lb' for the abbreviation of pound weight: the original showed lb with a horizontal line crossing to join the top of the letters.

Spelling of fouloir was corrected in the second paragraph of B(*b*) "The grapes were crushed in a foulior-egrappoir".

The name of the grape variety Muscat Madresfield Court was shortened to Muscat Madresfield in the chart on page 30 for formatting purposes.

If you have any questions concerning the original document or the accuracy of any part of the transcription please do not hesitate to contact Peter F May whose email address is peter@pinotage.org.

Hanepoot Jam – delicious on scones!

Glossary

Almeira — a table grape that is still grown in South Africa.

Aum — approximately 32 imperial gallons, (145.5 litres). One quarter of a leaguer.

Balling — a scale used to estimate sugar content in grape juice, from which the potential alcohol of the finished wine can easily be calculated. Balling is virtually identical to Brix. One degree Balling equates to one percent of sugar content. 24 degrees Balling would give a dry wine of around 13.2% alcohol by volume.

Barlinka — the variety discovered in 1909 by Perold near the village of Novi, on the Mediterranean coast west of Algiers in North Africa, and planted in the Cape in 1910. Barlinka has been a great success justifying Perold's recommendation in his 1916 report. This black table grape is known as 'Mr Reliable' and is one of the top twelve varieties grown today, according to the South African Table Grape Industry, with "bunches ripening well on the vine for a late harvest taste experience", it is "crunchy with good eating quality and has an excellent shelf life."

Bastardo do Castello — an almost vanished variety in the Cape with just 0.03 hectares planted, a figure that has remained stable for the past decade.

Bastardo do Menudo — a variety that has not been grown in the Cape for many years

Black Spanish — Perold was referring to a table grape variety rather than the present day synonym for the American Jacquez variety. In Perold's 1927 book *A Treatise on Viticulture* he names the variety as Black Alicante with Black Spanish as one of its synonyms, the others being: "Alicante, Black Lisbon, Black Portugal, Black St Peter's, Black Tokay, St Peter's etc". Alicante is also a synonym for Grenache Noir but it is clear this grape is not Grenache as Perold has separate entries for Black Spanish and Grenache in his later Treatise. Neither Black Spanish nor any of its synonyms appear on the list of table grape varieties currently grown in the South Africa. Interestingly, Black St Peter's was an alias of Zinfandel in 1870's America, where the grape was first grown for the table, but Zinfandel is not mentioned in Perold's Treatise.

Brouillis — a French term used in Cognac, France, for the cloudy liquid with an alcohol volume of 28 to 32% resulting from the first distillation. This liquid is then fermented a second time to produce the final brandy with an alcohol volume of around 70%.

Cartier — an early French hydrometer used to measure the amount of sugar in a solution in order to calculate potential alcohol

Cazenave — an Italian variation, suited to fertile soils, of Guyot vine trellising.

Cinsaut — see the glossary entry for Hermitage.

Claret — a British name, dating from the 15th century, for the red wines of Bordeaux, France. Perold used 'claret' to describe wines of a similar style though not necessarily from the same grape varieties.

Codega — name used in Portugal's Port producing Douro region for a white grape variety elsewhere known as Roupeiro. None currently growing in South Africa.

Colombard — now spelled Columbar in South Africa where it is the third most planted variety, after Chenin Blanc and Cabernet Sauvignon, with almost 12,000 hectares planted. But you rarely see the name on a bottle of wine because nearly all of it goes to brandy production.

Covent Garden — Britain's premier fruit and vegetable market was located in central London close to the River Thames, a little down river from the Houses of Parliament. The market moved to a new location out of the centre in 1974 and the original attractive restored Italianite market site is now a major tourist attraction famous for street entertainers and a selection of restaurants, shops and museums.

Flowers of Wine — see Mycoderma vini.

Folle Blanche — Perold recommends this grape as the best for brandy mentioning that it is the variety grown to make Cognac. However after phylloxera necessitated replanting vineyards around the end of the 19th Century Ugni Blanc (known by Perold as St Emilion) was favoured because of its resistance to powdery mildew and grey rot. Folle Blanche is now a very minor grape in France though some is still grown in Armagnac. There are no documented plantings in South Africa.

Fouloir-égrappoir — a machine that destems and crushes grapes.

Frontignac — Muscat de Frontignan. See glossary entry for Muscadel.

Gallon — Perold used the imperial gallon, which equals 4.54609 Litres

Grenache Noir — Grenache, or Garnacha in its Spanish homeland, is one of the world's most planted grape varieties. Little is grown in South Africa but plantings have been increasing with a more than four-fold growth in the past decade to 170Ha.

Greengrape — Local synonym for Semillon. Semillon was one of the earliest varieties brought to the Cape and for a long time was the most widely planted. It is likely that is bright green foliage gained it the name Greengrape and it was for generations *the* white grape variety. There are some rare strains that bear red grapes. These were known as Red Greengrapes to the confusion of visitors who asked about them. In the past few years some Red Greengrape vines have been discovered growing in very old vineyards and there are plans to make a varietal wine from them. Current plantings of Semillon are minimal, around 1% of vineyard plantings.

Guyot — widely used vine training system popularised by Jules Guyot in the 19th century.

Ha — abbreviation for Hectare: an area measuring 100 metres by 100 metres.

Halfaums — a half-aum (also spelled aam) was a measure of liquid of approximately 16 imperial gallons, (72.7 litres); also a barrel of that capacity

Hanepoot — the still current South African name for the large yellow Muscat grape of the variety Muscat d'Alexandrie. The grape is grown for dessert wines but at harvest time large trays of the succulent golden bunches are sold at the roadside and jars of delicious Hanepoot jams can be found in supermarkets and country stores. In his later book *A Treatise on Viticulture* Perold gives the explanation that Hanepoot is a corruption of Hane Kloot, meaning the testicles of a cockerel, which the grape was jokingly said to resemble. My knowledge of this bird begins and ends at the dinner table so I am unable to comment.

Hermitage — the South African synonym for Cinsaut (spelled Cinsault in France) at that time. Perold knew full well that they were one and the same as he was the person that made the identification. The variety was grown as a table grape for export and it was, in Perold's time, the most widely planted variety for red wine. In his report he uses the name Cinsaut just once, in the table on page 32.

Hock — British name dating from the 17th century for light German white wines from the Rhine, supposedly derived from Hoccheim.

Jacquez — an American vine widely used in South Africa at that time as a rootstock. Currently used to produce wine in France (unofficially) and in the USA, especially Texas where it is better known as Black Spanish or Lenoir. One of the 'legends' investigated in my book *PINOTAGE: Behind the Legends of South Africa's Own Wine* is the persistent rumour that Jacquez is one of the parents of the Pinotage variety following an accidental fertilisation in Perold's experimental vineyard.

lb — abbreviation for pound weight. One imperial pound weighs the same as 0.45359 kilograms.

Leaguer — 128 Imperial gallons, 581.9 litres. A leaguer consisted of 4 Aums or 16 Ankers. One Anker was 8 Imperial gallons (36.369 litres)

Malvasia Preta — black variety: one of the eighty-two varieties traditionally permitted for use in Port. Not listed under its own name in South Africa's official statistics but it might be included under the heading 'Port varieties' which shows 3.13 Ha.

Malvasia Rey — white variety: one of the eighty-two varieties traditionally permitted for use in Port. Not listed under its own name in South Africa's official statistics but it is probably included under the heading 'Port varieties' which shows 3.13 Ha. South African port specialist Allesveloren Estate currently grows Malvasia Rey for use in their fortified wines.

Money — in 1916 the Cape was using the British currency system based on the Pound Sterling. One pound (£ or L) contained 20 shillings (s) and each shilling consisted of 12 pennies (d). The abbreviations of £ s d dates back to Roman times and originally referred to Libra, Solidus and Denarius.

Mourisco de Semente — black variety: one of the eighty-two varieties traditionally permitted for use in Port but very rare. None are grown currently in South Africa.

Mourisco tinto — synonym for Marufo, a black variety and one of the eighty-two varieties traditionally permitted for use in Port although very rare. None is grown currently in South Africa.

Muscadel — Muscadel is the name used in South Africa for Muscat de Frontignan (also known as Muscat Blanc a Petite Grains and several other synonyms). There are white and red versions of this ancient variety and lots of confusion. Perold mentions in the same sentence Red Muscadel and Frontignac (his abbreviation of Muscat de Frontignan of Frontignac). Currently South Africa appears to use Muscadel when differentiating the red berried strain and Frontignan for the white berried and I think Perold also was. There are currently 684 Ha of Frontignac and 364 Ha of Red Muscadel growing in the Cape.

Mycoderma vini — a film-forming yeast that appears on the surface of wines. Perold here is equating this with the beneficial flor that forms on Sherry.

Naloop — the tailings; the last liquid obtained after the rest of the distillate has been acquired.

Ohanez — synonym of Almeira, a table grape variety still grown in the Cape.

Pedro Jimenez — nowadays spelled as Pedro Ximinez, and commonly called 'PX' this grape is grown in Spain primarily for Sherry. No PX is grown currently in South Africa. However Perold notes after Pedro Jimenez '(The False Pedro)'. The Andalucia variety Pedro Luis was known as False Pedro in the Cape and is still grown, although plantings have dropped by 100ha in the past decade to just 3.7ha. and it appears from Perold's Treatise that the variety then known as Pedro Jimenez was actually Pedro Luis.

Pontac — is a rare teinturer variety, meaning it has red flesh and juice. It was one of the first varieties planted and was used in the famous sweet Constantia wines. The worlds' last varietal Pontac was the 1998 vintage made by Hartenberg Estate in Stellenbosch who then pulled up the vines as they were diseased. Pontac still grows in the Cape where its grapes are used to add colour to blends and in the production of 'port' wines. However plantings have halved in the past decade till there are just 3.95Ha left. It seems a pity such a historic variety is being allowed to vanish.

Saccharometer — a hydrometer used to measure the amount of sugar in a solution.

Saint Emilion — was a synonym used in Cognac for Ugni Blanc, a very widely planted variety in France and Italy, where it is known as Trebbiano. In South Africa its vineyard area shrunk by more than two thirds in the past decade to just 66.4 hectares.

Stein — in 1916 it was thought to be a grape variety unique to South Africa and one of the first to be grown in the Cape, although Perold had doubts and thought it might be related to Sauvignon Blanc. It wasn't until 1963 that the variety was finally and incontrovertibly identified as Chenin Blanc by Professor Orffer, Perold's student and later successor as Professor of Viticulture at Stellenbosch University. Perold uses the spelling Stein but that later became Steen, a name that has now been dropped in South Africa in favour of Chenin Blanc. To get really confusing, there is a wine type in South Africa known as Stein which is a cheap semi-sweet blended white wine usually made predominately from Chenin Blanc. Chenin has long been the most planted variety in South Africa although area planted to it is reducing year by year as farmers convert to red varieties. Much of Chenin goes to brandy production but there are stunning varietal versions in dry, sweet, wooded and unwooded styles. Currently 18.7 thousand hectares, or about 18% of vineyard area, is planted with Chenin Blanc and the Cape grows more Chenin than the Loire, its original home.

Red Muscadel — see the glossary entry for Muscadel.

Stukvat — a large wooden wine barrel, literally a vat made from wooden sticks (or staves), rather than concrete. In Perold's day stukvats commonly had a capacity of 2,500 — 5000 litres and lay on their side. Their access hole was distinctively shaped like an inverted letter U. The term stukvat is still in use for large wooden vats. These days they are often set upright and are open-topped and used for fermentation.

Supernatant — the liquid lying above a solid residue.

Tinto Cao — one of the finest varieties for Port, though not now widely grown in Portugal. None currently listed growing in South Africa.

Tinta Francisca — black variety: one of the eighty-two varieties traditionally permitted for use in Port. There are 1.89 Ha currently listed growing in South Africa

Tinta Roriz — black variety: one of the eighty-two varieties traditionally permitted for use in Port. Tinta Roriz is a Portuguese synonym for the Spanish variety Tempranillo and there are 19.8 Ha of Tempranillo currently growing in South Africa. Plantings have slightly increased over the last decade, presumably for use in table wines.

Touriga — there are two Portuguese black grape varieties with the prefix Touriga: Nacional and Francesca. Touriga Nacional is listed as currently growing in South Africa. There are 89Ha of Nacional, a three-fold increase in the past decade.

White Crystal — table grape no longer grown in the Cape.

White French — South African synonym for Palomino, a Spanish variety used for making Sherry. It was widely planted in the Cape. As recently as 1994 it was the fourth most planted wine grape but by 2009 it had slid to 23rd position with just 330 hectares, presumably as a result of the decline of demand for sherry-style wines and the attraction of more profitable red wine grape varieties. Perold notes in this report that White French is 'practically identical' to Palomino and he writes Palomino(?) as a synonym of White French in his 1927 Treatise. Prior to DNA testing identification of grape vines relied on comparing leaves, fruit and growing times and, because there are sometimes distinct differences between different clones of the same variety, it was often a long time before suspicions became certainties.

Witzenberg – a wine growing area now focused around the town of Tulbagh.

Bibliography

Kenney, R U, 'Abraham Izak Perold – Wegwyser van ons wingerdbou', Human & Rousseau (Kaapstad), 1981, Cape Town

Kohler, C W H, 'The Memoirs of Kohler of the K.W.V.', Hurst & Blackett, 1946, London

May, P F, 'PINOTAGE: Behind the Legends of South Africa's Own Wine', Inform & Enlighten Ltd, 2009, St Albans

Perold, A I, 'A Treatise on Viticulture', MacMillan & Co, 1927, London

Pongracz, D.P, 'Rootstocks for Grape-Vines', David Phillip Publisher, 1983, Cape Town

Robinson, J, (Editor), 'The Oxford Companion to Wine (Third Edition)', Oxford University Press, 2006, Oxford.

———————— 'Vines, Grapes & Wines', Mitchell Beazley, 1986, London

SATGI South African Table Grape Industry Partnership, 'South African Grape Calendar', www.satgi.co.za (accessed 23 February 2011)

Whitehead, C & **Uren, N**, 'Statistics of Wine-Grape Vines as at November 2009', SA Wines Information & Systems, 2010, Paarl

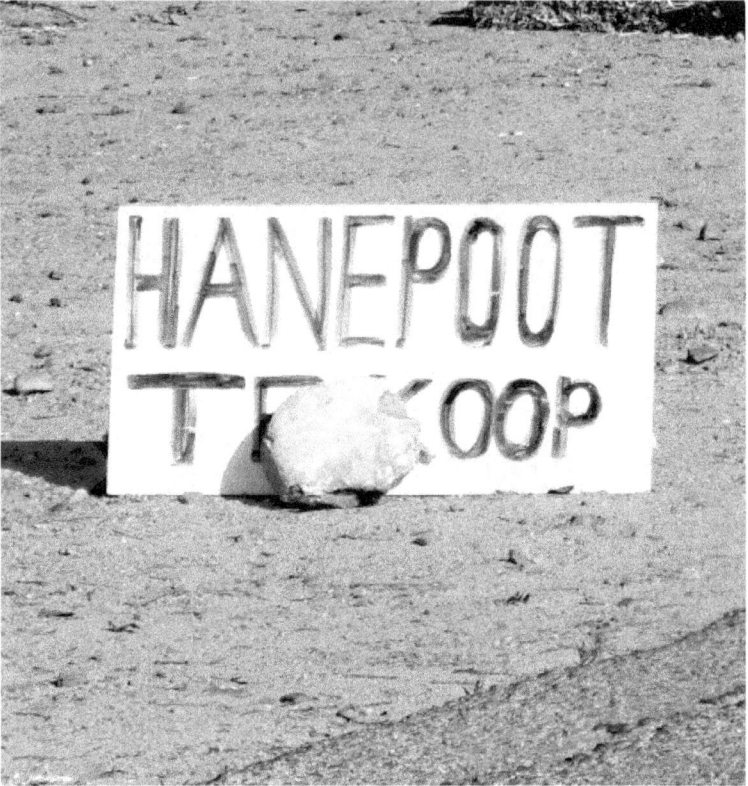

Hanepoot for Sale

Street trader's sign advertising freshly picked Hanepoot
grapes for the table at the roadside in Stellenbosch.

Index

Hanepoot vines growing in Delheim's vineyards on the
slopes of Stellenbosch's Simonsberg mountain.

Peter F May

Peter F May is founder of The Pinotage Club at www.pinotage.org and an Honorary Member of the producers Pinotage Association. He has been enthusiastic about Dr Perold's gift to the world since he first visited South Africa in 1996 and has returned to the Cape wine lands every year since then.

He sat Wine & Spirit Education Trust courses gaining the WSET Certificate and then the WSET Higher Certificate with Distinction in 1982. In 2003 passed as an lecturer for The Cape Wine Academy, South Africa's official wine education body.

In February 2004 he was awarded Honorary Membership of the producers Pinotage Association. He has been an Associate Judge at the International Wine Challenge in London, judged at The South Africa National Wine Show 'Veritas' competition, twice at the ABSA/Pinotage Association 'Top 10' Pinotage Competition and was on the WINE magazine Sauvignon Blanc tasting panel.

Peter is a member of The Circle of Wine Writers. His articles have appeared in several publications and websites. In 2005 he was commissioned by Quirk Books, Philadelphia, to write *Marilyn Merlot & The Naked Grape* and in 2009 his book *PINOTAGE: Behind the Legends of South Africa's Own Wine* was published.

He lives in St Albans, England.

PINOTAGE: *Behind the Legends of South Africa's Own Wine*

by **Peter F May**

During researches in South Africa author Peter F May was told information that differed from the standard definition of Pinotage in text books. Turning detective, May investigated various legends about Pinotage's parentage and origins.

"I felt like Sherlock Holmes," says May "as winemakers told me things in confidence that contradicted everything I'd read about Pinotage."

May travelled to four continents to interview winemakers and winery owners for the book which details how Pinotage is grown, made and marketed. As well as covering growing, making and marketing Pinotage in South Africa, he provides a comprehensive review of Pinotage in other countries.

"Pinotage is a wine of great importance in its homeland that is getting increasing international attention and yet there was little reliable information available", says May. "Since no-one was doing so, I decided to write a book that would place the facts on record and nail the rumours. I ended with a book which is part mystery, part history, part travel book and yet all about wine."

Paperback: 248 pages
ISBN-13: 978-0956152305
Also available from Amazon as a Kindle ebook

Marilyn Merlot and the Naked Grape:
Odd Wines from Around the World

by

Peter F May

Marilyn Merlot and the Naked Grape is an amusing and entertaining book that features more than 100 full colour photographs of unusual, weird and interesting wine labels.

Author Peter F May believes wine should be fun, and this book celebrates the quirky and odd. But among the humour there is solid wine information. You'll learn why many red Shiraz wines now contain some white Viognier and what 'Contains Sulphites' means as well as why older women ask for 'the big one' instead of naming the wine they want and what happens when Rude Girl gets warm.

Winemakers, winery owners, label designers and artists have revealed to Peter the secrets behind their labels. When you've finished laughing there is information about how to remove wine labels, tasting notes and contact details for wines featured, and a comprehensive glossary.

Published by Quirk Books

256 full colour pages

Introduction by Robin Garr

ISBN-13: 978-1594740992

Roman Sunset

a novel by

Elizabeth May

350 years of civilization suddenly collapsed, almost overnight. Trade, government, education and the rule of law ceased.

This was Britain at the beginning of the fifth century. As Rome's legions departed to fight in Europe, opportunist raiders took advantage of the wealth left behind, unguarded. Invaders devastated rich farmlands, burning carefully tended crops, cherry picking healthy Britons for use as slaves and ruthlessly slaying anyone else in their path.

Roman Sunset rings with the cries of human voices, carrying across the centuries. Retired Roman soldiers after years of service face a battle they feel they cannot win. Desperately seeking shelter in a weathered cavalry fort they watch as all they know burns. A make-shift community forms as other refugees from the violent storm of battle gather for safety. They know it is not a matter of if the raiders will return, but when. Together they must put aside their differences, combine their skills and claw a path of survival in a new, lawless environment.

Paperback: 268 pages

ISBN-13:978-1430309376

Also available from Amazon as a Kindle ebook

Roman Twilight

a novel by

Elizabeth May

Five years have passed since Quintus fought his last battle. Since then he has been breeding horses. Then an old friend's death gives him an urge to travel and see the Roman Empire, which he had served so faithfully, one more time.

His itchy feet take him through Western Europe during the Fifth century. A year on the road will see him go from honoured old soldier to slave and then back to respected general.

In his adventures he meets the characters who shaped those years: St Patrick, the Irish king Niall of the Nine Hostages, King Arthur's father and the ancestors of the founders of France. Europe is in upheaval. Goths, Franks and Huns are all pushing west while the Irish push east. Meanwhile what is left of the Roman Empire is in rebellion.

Can the old general save them from themselves?

Paperback: 228 pages

ISBN-13: 978-1446110522

Also available from Amazon as a Kindle ebook

www.ingramcontent.com/pod-product-compliance
Lightning Source LLC
Chambersburg PA
CBHW021211020426
42331CB00003B/301